John Potts

Memorials of the life of Edward & Lydia Ann Jackson

With discourses preached in the Centenary Church

John Potts

Memorials of the life of Edward & Lydia Ann Jackson
With discourses preached in the Centenary Church

ISBN/EAN: 9783337259709

Printed in Europe, USA, Canada, Australia, Japan

Cover: Foto ©Lupo / pixelio.de

More available books at **www.hansebooks.com**

MEMORIALS

OF THE LIFE OF

Edward & Lydia Ann Jackson,

BY N. BURWASH.

With Discourses

Preached in the Centenary Church, Hamilton, on the occasion of their
death, by the

Revs. W. J. HUNTER and JOHN POTTS.

.

TORONTO:

S. ROSE, METHODIST BOOK ROOM, KING ST. EAST.

1876.

PREFACE.

"WHEREVER, in our day, the attempt is made
to verify the achievements of heroic men,
the individuality of the men themselves becomes the
first subject of inquiry. Biography is, perhaps, the
most assiduously cultivated of all the departments
of serious literature in our age. But what is a
biography? Is it simply the chronological recapitu-
lation of a series of events? the enumeration of the
triumphs of a conqueror, of the writings of an
author, of the discoveries of a man of science, of
the principles of a thinker, the miracles of a saint?
Nay, is it not rather primarily the progressive
picture of the inner life of a man? the history of
the education which he first received, as well as of
that which he subsequently gave himself ere he became, in fine, the educator of his generation? It is

the story of the way in which he grew into what he ultimately was; it is the discovery of the true nature of his originality, of the tendencies of his mind, the aim of his efforts, the modes of his working; it is, in a word, the great drama of the contest of a heroic will, whether with the force of inertia or with the active resistance of traditional authority."*

It might be thought that such an ideal of biography is suitable for men of great mark in public affairs, for the warrior, the statesman, the philosopher, or the divine; but not for the less brilliant record of men who have followed the common callings of life. But we think not so. The serious aim of biography must always be the instruction of those who are just entering life. Scarcely one in a thousand of these can engage in those more public and prominent spheres of action. The great majority of men in every age must be content with the quiet industries of trade and agriculture, as furnishing the prime necessaries of life. And if in these pursuits the highest excellence of character may be developed, and if with these humbler toils the very highest aims of life may be combined, then the history of such development and the exhibition of such noble

* Reuss, Hist. of Theol. in the Apost. Age.

aims are the very best examples for universal instruction. It is at least noteworthy that the beautiful and impressive biographical sketches of the Bible are largely drawn from common life.

But such biographies are, of all others, the most difficult to write, not from lack of interest in the subject, but from the difficulty of obtaining the necessary materials. The biographer cannot avail himself of the license of the novelist, and supply from the general study of humanity a warp of incident into which he may weave his ideal character. Public men lead a life full of *recorded* incident. The incidents of private life are lost to memory because, like the drops of rain, they so much resemble each other. And yet these incidents often touch the deepest springs of our nature, and thus, as well as by their frequent repetition, mould the character most powerfully. In the brief biography which we herewith present, we have been especially unfortunate in this respect. When the idea of a memoir of Edward Jackson was first suggested, Mrs. Jackson was still surviving; but the sorrow of bereavement was pressing so heavily that we could not add to it by asking her to recount the story of their past life. Ere this only opportunity came, she, too, was suddenly gone, and the children who might have remembered much had all gone before, and we found only a few fragments left of what had else been a sumptuous feast. On this account we are forced to crave indulgence for the imperfection of this work, We have been able to touch but one or two more prominent points in the spiritual growth of two persons whom of all others whom we have known we would feel disposed to hold up for the admiration and imitation of our generation.

There has been left us, however, one other thing to do. The artist has before him a beautiful flower. He may know nothing of the soil on which it has grown, of the sunshine and rain which have nourished it, or of the gardener's skill which hath nurtured it. The secret chemism by which crude matter has been transformed into such beauty may be altogether beyond his ken. But he can produce a life-like picture of the beauteous finished thing which lies before him. To our failure in this work we must humbly confess our lack of skill.

It affords us great pleasure to be able to associate with this brief memoir the discourse preached by the Rev. W. J. Hunter on the occasion of the decease of Mr. Jackson, and that preached by the Rev. J. Potts on the decease of Mrs. Jackson.

In Memoriam.

In Memoriam.

EDWARD AND LYDIA ANN JACKSON.

I N the year 1789, Jesse Lee visited New England, and Methodist zeal came in contact with stern Puritan orthodoxy. Although but twenty-three years had passed since the first Methodist sermon had been preached in America, and the first little society formed in New York, Methodism had already largely possessed itself of the continent. Baltimore, Philadelphia, and New York were now important centres. The labours of the great missionary bishop, Asbury, extended from the Carolinas to New York ; and this very year, pioneers were pushing across the St. Lawrence into Canada, and over the Alleghanies into Kentucky and Tennessee. New England had waited so long for her turn, probably on the principle of John Wesley, " Go to those that need you most."

Her people had long been reputed for religion and morality, a reputation which had not been gained by mere externalism. In the first half of the century revivals of wondrous extent and power had blessed the Puritan Churches, and many who had known Jonathan Edwards and George Whitfield were still living. But since their time there had been considerable spiritual declension, and the rising generation had generally conceived the strongest prejudices against all religious excitement. However, on his first tour around this newly-formed New England circuit, Lee found a chosen few, who, at an earlier day or in other lands, had experienced the joys of a present salvation, and were ready to welcome those who preached that blessed doctrine. Foremost among those was Aaron Sanford, the first male member of the Methodist Church in New England. The Sanford family, or families, (for there seem to have been at least two brothers,) appear to have emigrated from England a year or two before, where it is supposed Aaron was converted under the preaching of Wesley himself. The family settled in Redding, Connecticut, and here, on his second Sabbath, Lee found this boy ready to welcome Methodism, and to become the pioneer Methodist layman of New England. He afterwards became a local preacher, and was noted as a man of deep piety and great spiritual power, the instrument in God's hands of the conversion of many souls. Through his influence both branches of the Sanford family became associated with the Methodist Church. The descendants of these early Methodist families have spread widely through the United States and Canada, and to-day are to be found in the pulpit and the college chair, as well as in commercial life, distinguished by great energy and integrity of character and remarkable business ability. The old patriarch himself is also still living to tell the story of that former day. Nearly a century has multiplied the seed sown on the two Sabbaths, the first at Stratford and the second at Redding. Among the garnered fruits are Nathan and Heman Bangs, Lydia Ann Sanford, and Edward Jackson.

The Jackson family were Episcopalians, and had no direct connection with Methodism before the conversion of Edward Jackson. Judging, however, from his subsequent career, he must have been educated after the style of the good old-fashioned churchman, in the fear of God and the practice of virtue. He was born in Redding, on the 20th of April, 1799. His education at school, and as an apprentice, were such as would enable him to earn his livelihood, as his family was without wealth. His brilliant social qualities and engaging person, must have rendered him one of the most agreeable of youthful companions.

He did not altogether escape the dangers and temptations to which such qualities expose a young man. But early training and the love of a truly noble and virtuous woman, were influences in the hand of God to restrain and guide him until regenerating grace renewed and established his goings. This woman was Lydia Ann Sanford, of the family we have just described. She was born in Redding, March 17th, 1804, and so was five years his junior. She was nurtured under the influences of Methodism.. Her childhood was spent within a stone's throw of Aaron Sanford's house, where the Methodist meetings were held in those early days. The old house is still standing, with a curious partition hinged to the ceiling and fastened up by a button, a device by which the two principal rooms were thrown into one to accommodate the worshippers on the Sabbath. Her mother was here converted, and, while the daughter was still young, died in the faith, strengthened in her last hours by the prayers and exhortations of her godly relative. The daughter was gifted with more than ordinary talent and beauty, and her family were now rapidly rising to wealth and social position. Her ambitious brothers were therefore not a little disappointed to see their favourite sister disposed to wed a man who, whatever his personal attractions, had only his hands, head, and heart, upon which to depend for his fortune. However, that fine womanly instinct, which in after years rendered her judgment of men and motives so trustworthy, stood her in good stead at this important juncture, and under its influence, in 1826 she united her lot with Edward Jackson. It was not many years before the wealth which she discerned in her husband placed her in a position of affluence and social respectability worthy of the sacrifice which she had made for him, and her brothers were foremost to acknowledge the fact and to rejoice in her prosperity.

Leaving friends and native place behind them, they at once turned their faces westward, to seek such fortune as God had in store for them. They carried with them only a little household furniture, the implements of his trade, and what money was barely sufficient for the journey. At this time thousands were moving westward; Ohio, Illinois, Michigan, and Canada were all presenting their attractions. What conscious influence directed the way of our young travellers we know not. It scarcely could have been political considerations; for though they became true and loyal citizens of their adopted country, and did not, like many, carry off the wealth there gotten to spend it elsewhere, yet they ever retained a sincere regard for the land of their nativity. Probably it may have been commercial reasons. There was at that time scarcely a single trader in tinware in the western peninsula of Canada, and the rich furs of our northern climate afforded an opportunity for barter not to be obtained elsewhere. If such were the expectations of Mr. Jackson, the results certainly proved the wisdom of his venture. But however this might be, it is certain that the God of their fathers was directing the way of His children's children, though as yet unknown to them. There were great blessings in store for them, and a great work for them to do in this new country, and for these they were hither led.

Towards the end of autumn they landed in Niagara. The sale of some furniture provided the means to purchase a small stock of material, and the young man immediately set to work. His energy and industry soon commanded confidence, and a gentleman loaned him one hundred dollars for the enlargement of his stock. Before fifteen months, this was repaid, a little capital saved, and the foundations of all their future commercial prosperity secured by the economy and industry of the first year of their married life. They then removed to Ancaster, at the head of the lake, as a more convenient centre for a trade which was henceforth to be pushed northward and westward to all the new settlements of the peninsula. On their journey thither they passed through Hamilton. There were then two farm houses with scanty clearing in a magnificent forest, stretching from Burlington Bay to the summit of the mountain. But this place, with immediate water communication to all the East, was destined to be the permanent commercial centre, and thither, early in 1830, Mr. Jackson removed, purchased a lot, and finally established his business. Already the extent of his trade was such as to afford employment for five or six young men. The first list included the following names :—William , Wheeler, now of Chicago ; the late Hiram Piper, of Toronto ; Murray Anderson, of London ; and Dennis Moore, of Hamilton, the latter but fifteen years of age. These young men were received into his family, and enjoyed all the advantages of his henceforth Christian home. Subsequently they all became active partners of Mr. Jackson in various extensions of his business. The aggregate property accumulated by them has amounted to more than a million dollars. And in almost every instance the foundation of all their future success was laid during this period of intimate relationship, social as well as commercial, with Mr. and Mrs. Jackson. Probably scarcely another commercial house in the country could produce a similar record.

The year 1832 was no ordinary one in the history of Canadian Methodism. The terrible scourge of cholera, which passed over this, in common with

other lands, had produced unusual seriousness in the
minds of the people. The two branches of Methodism
had just succeeded in overcoming the prejudices which
had separated them, and the arrangements for the
first union were completed. With a deep sense of
their responsibility, and with renewed courage for
their work, the ministers of our Church addressed
themselves in the autumn of that year to labour for
the salvation of souls. Early in the year we hear of
great revivals all round our narrow frontier country,
from Niagara to Rideau. In October there had
already been some forty added to the Church in
Hamilton, and before the end of the year there were
a hundred converts in the village of six hundred inhabitants. The total reported increase of the year
was 1217, nearly ten per cent. on the membership of
the previous year. The ministers labouring in
Hamilton were James Evans and Edwy Ryerson.
The meetings were held in the old King St. Church,
at that time the only place of worship in the village.
Mrs. Jackson, in a strange land, had not forgotten
the Methodist associations of her childhood, and with
this sanctuary she had connected herself on coming to
the place. When the special services commenced, Mr.
Jackson was absent from home on business. She,
however, taking with her Mr. Moore as her escort,
found her way regularly over the half mile of swamp

between her house and the church. Already God's Spirit was striving powerfully with her, and the convictions of her own heart she laboured earnestly to impress on the boy who walked with her to and from the house of prayer. Before long she presented herself at the altar as a penitent, and there soon found peace in believing. This was in the beginning of February, 1833. The next week Mr. Jackson returned home. At once his converted wife, true to the instincts of old-fashioned Methodism, set herself to work for his conversion. We shall describe their first interview in his own words, used at a fellowship-meeting a few weeks later.

" My bosom companion met me, when I got home, on her knees, and, weeping, entreated me to seek religion. I had never prayed in my life. I was a profane man and fond of ungodly associates. I had embraced the principles of Universalism. But five minutes' conviction of the Holy Spirit scattered all these, and I then determined to serve God and seek salvation."

That night he accompanied his wife to the meeting and took his seat in a convenient place, well forward. As soon as the invitation was given he arose, laid off his overcoat, and walked to the prayer-circle. Two or three days later, before he yet found peace, he addressed himself to Mr. Moore, who regularly attended the meetings, and was deeply serious. He elicited from him his convictions, and offered to accompany him to the altar, and that night the two, who were to be so many years associated in business and Christian work, were found bowed together as penitents. The blessing still tarried. But a few days later Mr. Jackson was alone in his shop, walking to and fro behind the counter, meditating upon his position. He was in great perplexity. He felt the responsibility of the profession to which he had engaged himself, and it seemed greater than he was able to bear before his men and his former ungodly associates. The way of faith, too, seemed dark, an impenetrable mystery. Out of this distress he tried to look up to God, when like a flash of light the witness of sonship was given, and his heart was filled with joy and praise. In a short time not only Moore, but Anderson, and nearly all the other young men in the shop were converted, and there was indeed a happy Christian household.

At once Mr. Jackson assumed that foremost position in Christian labour and influence for which his talents fitted him. He learned that there was a debt on the parsonage of $600, for which the ministers were personally responsible. With some friends he assumed the obligation, and made an effort to raise the needed money. All the inmates of the house presented their contributions, the youngest, Moore, bringing a sovereign, his entire savings from his apprentice wages, and offering it to the cause of God. A thousand-fold return he has since reaped from this first precious investment.

All the enterprises of the Church, her missions, her college then just building, as well as her local interests, now presented their claims to Mr. Jackson, and nobly did he respond to them. But the financial interests of the Church were far from being his sole concern. The great extension of the Church membership had created a necessity for new classes and leaders. The newly organized class to which Mr. and Mrs. Jackson were attached, found its place of meeting in their own house. For some weeks the minister himself acted as leader. As the pressing duties of the close of Conference year came on, he sought release, and nominated a brother Clement, who declined. Then Mr. Jackson was nominated, and struggling against reluctance and fear he accepted, and nobly filled the office in that class for forty years. The class continued to meet in his own house until the erection of the McNab St. Church, in 1851.

The united career of our friends, for the next twenty-five years, ran in a somewhat even course, without those incidents which make turning points in life. Ability and industry in commerce in that interval accumulated a princely fortune. The talents and early training of both enabled them to fill, with no ordinary grace and dignity, the position in society which they were now called to occupy, and they were honoured and respected as among the excellent of the earth. Meantime their magnificent home was still the home of the humble Methodist preacher. The class-meeting and prayer-meeting were as highly prized and as faithfully attended as in early days. They warmly sympathized with all the interests of the Church, and in some of the most trying emergencies through which Canadian Methodism passed, Edward Jackson with his means, his commercial credit, his counsel, and his influence, was the right-hand supporter of those who were called to guide the ship. Their domestic life was not without its shadows. The little blossoms of hope, son and daughter, lent by their Father in Heaven, were soon called back, and but one lovely flower was left. Mr. Jackson's health was often feeble, and sometimes he was driven, by our severe climate, to spend the winters in the South. But these shadows were lightened by many blessings. They had the satisfaction of seeing many young men and two young ladies trained up in their home to lives of promise and usefulness. The Church of their choice, and the city of their abode, were sharing in the general prosperity of the country.

Above all, their home was lightened by the presence
of a remaining child, who more than satisfied all
their fondest hopes. Gifted by nature with the
soundest judgment, and engaging person and man-
ners, she added to the refinement of the highest
culture the most tender affections, and the most conscientious piety. Seven years after her decease, when
it was our privilege to become a member of this
household, we found many a book in the library with
marginal notes in her hand-writing, testifying to her
intellectual culture and fervid piety. And when, in
1857, her parents saw her happily married to one
worthy of her affections, it would seem as if their
cup of earthly bliss were full.

But the Master was already saying unto them, " I
will show you greater things than these." These
greater things were to purify their hearts as gold is
tried by fire.

By one sudden stroke child and grandchild were
taken from them and laid together in the grave, and
their home left empty and desolate. This was indeed
the hour of extreme anguish, but they bowed their
hearts to it as to a father's chastening. To the outside world they seemed to shut themselves up with
their grief for weeks. But they were dwelling with
their God, humbly seeking strength to learn the
lessons of His rod. Day after day, known only to

their household attendants, they spent in the chamber of the departed, now bowed in earnest prayer, now walking to and fro with the Word of God in their hands. And when they came forth from their hours of sorrow, seclusion, and supplication, it was to a higher, grander Christian life than they had experienced ever before. Property, time, talents, influence, all were henceforth to be consecrated to God. A true estimate of the importance of this period of their religious history can only be formed from the activities of their subsequent life. But the following rules, which appear to have been adopted by Mrs. Jackson at this time, though drawn up probably by herself and her daughter during the preceding year, will show how entire was the consecration which she now made of herself to God.

RULES OF LIFE.

1. That the salvation of my soul shall be my first and great concern.

2. That I will never be ashamed of my religion, but will always avow it, when and where it may be proper so to do.

3. That I will always carefully speak the truth, and will never indulge in the very least equivocation, but always be both verbally and substantially correct, and to this end I will watch the meaning of all I utter.

4. That I will always be ready to confess a fault, or ask forgiveness for it, no matter what the character or position of the person against whom I have offended.

5. That I will do nothing to others which I would object to their doing to me. That I will never do anything which, if I saw committed by another, would cause him or her to fall in my esteem.

6. That as far as in me lies I will never do or be anything upon which I cannot confidingly and expectingly ask the blessing of God.

7. That when I have fixed a principle in my mind, I will never abandon it, whatever occurs, unless I am convinced it is a wrong one, or would involve me in bad consequences.

8. That in fulfilling a clear duty, or in the pursuit of a good and proper object, I will never allow myself to be overcome by any trials or difficulties whatever.

9. That I will daily study the Scriptures.

10. That I will encourage meditation on death and eternity.

11. That I will live to God with all my might while I do live. That I will strive never to engage in anything which I should shun if assured I was living the last hour of my life.

12. That I will decide nothing which is brought before my judgment until I have thoroughly examined it on every side. That what I have once decided shall be fixed and irrevocable. That I will take nothing for granted, but that I will endeavour to discover what is truth in reference to the smallest principles.

13. That upon all occasions I will discountenance improper levity and conversation, in whatever company I may be.

14. That I will carefully guard my temper, and never show the least symptom of impatient emotion, not even by an altered tone of voice, or expression of countenance. That I will do this even if from physical causes I feel fretful and uneasy, as no one else should suffer on my account.

15. That I will never speak crossly to servants, but be gentle and affectionate, which will gain my desires the sooner.

16. That my conversation shall be always in love, and as far as possible adapted to the tone of feeling of those with whom I converse. That I will never converse upon trifles, or self, or the failings or defects of others.

17. That I will never waste a moment.

18. That I will be temperate in eating and drinking.

19. That I will strictly guard against pride in dress, and every other of its manifestations.

20. That I will live only to serve God, and for the good of others, never seek my own pleasure or satisfaction at the expense of that of any one else, but, as far as possible, forget that there is a self to please.

21. That I will love my dear husband with all my might, and do everything in my power (no matter what the sacrifice required), to promote his happiness.

We have no such written record of the exercises of Mr. Jackson's heart at this time, but his subsequent actions, as well as remarks, occasionally dropt to most intimate friends, show that they were neither less deep nor permanent. His brethren in the Church have testified to us that henceforth he was a new man. Referring to this period in his life, he once said in our hearing, " I went with my Bible to the upper room, and when I came down I had a new heart, and felt that it was all right." Within the next two years his regular permanent contributions to the cause of God were quadrupled. About this time our missions on the Pacific Coast were founded under the charge of the Rev. E. Evans, D.D. The means at the disposal of the Society were limited, and to lay the foundations of our Church without disparagement by the side of the incoming denomination so munificently endowed by Miss Burdett Coutts, was no easy matter. Dr. Evans built in faith, becoming himself personally responsible for a considerable part of the cost of the church. As his liabilities were maturing, he wrote to Mr. Jackson, asking for aid. There was scarcely a day for delay if the answer was to return in time. Meantime the darkness thickened around the missionary. On the morning when his note matured, and he expected his name to be dishonoured at the bank, his only son was a corpse waiting for burial on the morrow. But that very morning came to the crushed man a letter from one whom God had likewise brought through tribulation, with $1,000 to meet the pressing note. To those thousand dollars five hundred more were added immediately afterwards, which were the proceeds of the sale of his deceased daughter's jewelry. And this last costly and precious gift was again nearly doubled by subscriptions obtained from friends in Hamilton.

The later years of the life of Mr. and Mrs. Jackson were devoted to a series of great Christian enterprises, with which their names will always be identified in the future. In these Mrs. Jackson appears not simply as the partner of her husband's

2

liberality. The inheritance left her by her father, at his death, had been so judiciously managed by her husband that it was now a handsome fortune, yielding her an income of more than a thousand a year, over which he always insisted that she should have absolute control. And when, hereafter, we see her name appearing for a succession of large gifts to the cause of God, they were gifts in her own right.

One of the first works in which we find them engaged was the foundation of the Wesleyan Female College, at Hamilton. In the success of this Institution, even as a commercial enterprise, Mr. Jackson had the strongest faith. He was by far the largest subscriber to the stock, ánd was the active, interested President of its Directorate till his death. The teachers and pupils of the school, in its early days of struggle, will also remember how generously the social courtesy of Mr. and Mrs. Jackson was extended to them, and how much this contributed to the pleasure of their residence in Hamilton.

For many years Mrs. Jackson had been associated with "The Hamilton Ladies' Orphan Asylum and Benevolent Society." As Treasurer and Directress, by careful management of its funds, by wise distribution of its charities, by personal appeals to the citizens on its behalf, as well as by her weekly visits to the home of the children, and many a pleasant treat provided for the little ones at her own residence, she contributed perhaps as largely as any other individual to the success of the Institution. There was no interest dearer to her heart than that of these destitute children, and it was a touching token of the affection with which she inspired them, to see the little ones with emblems of mourning solemnly and silently following her to the grave.

In the year 1866 Mr. Jackson set his heart upon the erection of a central Methodist church, in Hamilton, worthy of the cause and of the rapidly extending city. Enterprises of this kind were in progress at this time in all the great centres of Methodism in the United States. New York, Detroit, Chicago, Washington, and Boston had just completed or were building magnificent structures, centres of attraction and power and denominational influence. Hamilton was the first to extend this enterprise to our country. We had already, it is true, in Montreal, Kingston, Belleville, Toronto, and London, large, and some of them beautiful, churches. But these had grown up in the ordinary extension of the work, and not with a view to providing a denominational landmark in the city. It was no easy matter to inspire others with the enthusiasm which he himself felt for this work. They worshipped in a very comfortable and somewhat com-

modious church in a central part of the city, and
why should they expend an immense sum in building
anew? However, he was not to be discouraged by
ordinary difficulties. He led the way with a subscription hitherto unexampled in the church-building
of Canadian Methodism. He himself canvassed, not
the city, but the congregation, for subscriptions, for
he was determined that no one should be *asked* to
contirbute outside of their own congregation. Finally,
by the most active efforts he succeeded in bringing
the subscription list to a point at which the trustees
considered themselves justified in beginning to build,
and the corner-stone was laid by Mrs. Jackson,
shortly after Conference, 1866. Meanwhile the ladies
under her leadership were equally active, and had
accumulated a large sum for the complete furnishing
of the church as soon as it passed from the builders'
hands. After two years of the most watchful interest
and active effort, they had the satisfaction, in May,
1868, of seeing the magnificent sanctuary dedicated
to the worship of Almighty God by the Rev. Wm.
Morley Punshon, immediately on his arrival in this
country.

During these same years the Centenary movement,
the effort to remove the debt and to provide for the
endowment of Victoria College, and the removal of
the debt of the Missionary Society, as well as all the

ordinary local and general claims of the Church, received the hearty support and co-operation of Mr. and Mrs. Jackson, and drew upon their resources to the extent of thousands of dollars. They were also deeply interested in the movements on behalf of the freedmen of the Southern States, and contributed largely to several societies organized for that good work.

In 1871 an effort was made by our Church for the establishment of a theological department in Victoria College. This was a work in which Mr. Jackson had long felt a deep interest. He had been familiar with the history, and had rejoiced in the success of the Garrett Biblical Institute, of the M. E. Church, of the United States. The class of six young men who assembled at his house for instruction in the winter of '65 and '66, had enlisted his hearty sympathy, and he followed each of them in his subsequently successful ministerial career with a kind of paternal pride. Several young men had been assisted at College by his liberality, and by more than ordinary gifts and graces had shown how wisely he discerned men for the work. As soon as a more extensive work in this direction was presented to him he entered into it with all his heart. He did not feel justified in taking upon himself the entire financial burden, but contrived a plan by which the .

first chair in theology in the institution might be provided for. But this design was scarcely entered upon ere he heard the messenger calling for him. Being fully assured that the end was near, he at once set about making preparation for it. Few men less needed preparation. For years he had lived in the experience of a Christian joy and peace, simple, fervid, and fresh as that of a converted child. A present, happy faith in Christ, was his constant theme in the class-meeting and love-feast. His worldly affairs were in admirable order, and could scarcely be better arranged. It only remained that he should strengthen the heart of his sorrowing companion, and in consultation with her perfect the plans of work for God and the Church which were now beginning to engage his attention. The few weeks which remained were devoted to this work. Lying on his couch, suffering in body but clear in mind and strong in heart, he spent hours in quiet conversation with her. All important points were minutely considered, and the difficulties of her future provided for, so that in his departure she felt that she knew all that was in his heart.

At this time his friends were far from anticipating his speedy decease, but he was ready, and ere they were aware the hour had come. It was a beautiful Sabbath evening in July. The hour of worship was over, and the pastors, with a few privileged friends, had come to join in praise and prayer with the Lord's prisoner. After words of pleasant greeting, he himself led the way to the parlour, showed each one a seat, opened the piano, and asked Brother Benson to lead in his favourite hymn, " The power of prayer." They then kneeled together, and Brother Benson led in prayer. The aged saint was heard responding in fervent " Amens." Mr. Sanford, who was kneeling beside him, looked up, saw his face covered with a radiance of joy, and the next moment caught him in his arms, as the earthly tabernacle fell backwards, and the spirit was gone to the songs of the blest. He rested in Jesus July 14th, 1872, aged 73 years 2 months and 24 days.

The genial, graceful, intelligent countenance of this great and good man is before us still with vivid distinctness. But our language must utterly fail to describe his grand Christian character. Taking him all for all, he was the most perfect man we ever knew.

Pre-eminent in his religious character was his unaffected simplicity. His words were like the words of a child to his father, and his experience was always like the story of one, who, but yesterday had been converted. He never learned to use stale cant, and few could listen to his admonitions as a class-leader, full of plain, practical common sense, without being roused to appreciate the simple reality of the Christian life.

His integrity and veracity were of the highest order. His was the soul of honour and the spirit of truth. Every man who dealt with him knew how safely he might rely on his conscientious regard for the rights of others. He was not the man to speculate, which generally means to make money out of the losses of others. His property was accumulated by prudent foresight, and constant industry and economy. In the social circle he was a man of the most engaging qualities, and a universal favourite with the young. His keen humour and brilliant wit often excited their merriest laughter. But he was always gentlemanly, he used no slang, and condescended to no coarse vulgarity. No one, after his conversion, ever heard from him words of profane levity. He was a man of remarkable quickness of apprehension. His conclusions, which were generally sound, seemed to flash upon him like an intuition. This readiness of discernment gave him great power in directing the efforts of others. Father Carroll tells of sitting down with him at a meeting of church officials where the accounts of the treasurer seemed in inextricable confusion. Mr. Jackson himself did not put a pen to paper, but directed Mr. A. to reckon this, and Mr.

B. to reckon that, and in a few minutes, with the aid of half-a-dozen heads and pencils, he was able to present a plain and accurate statement of the whole affair. This power of directing others made him acknowledged leader wherever he appeared, and was, doubtless, one important cause of his success in life. These strong points of character were directed by a humanity which was universal in its sympathies, tempered by great humility and meekness, and sanctified by entire consecration to God.

Mrs. Jackson had scarcely become accustomed to the first keen sorrows of bereavement ere she addressed herself to the great work which her husband had committed to her. The objects contemplated were three,—first, to enlarge the endowment of the superannuated ministers' fund; second, to give a fresh impetus to the great mission work; third, to provide fully and permanently for the chair of theology in Victoria College. To do for these objects what they desired, required some $50,000. Mr. Jackson had himself devised $10,000 to the last-named work, but left the full accomplishment of his wishes to his wife. Her first aim was so to increase the estate left in her hands, as to make it sufficient both to meet the claims of kindred and to complete these great projects for the Church. For two years she devoted herself entirely to this, managing her affairs with the most rigid economy until, by the end of that time, she had added $25,000 to her capital. Her motives were understood by few. Some even insinuated that the spirit of avarice had taken possession of her. But in a quiet conversation with the writer, she explained the convictions of duty and the plans upon which she was acting. At the Conference, held in Hamilton, June, 1874, her end was attained. She then completed the execution of her husband's will, and of his further expressed desire as to the theological chair. She shortly after cancelled the temporary arrangement of her estate, by which she had provided against the contingency of death, and in her last will and testament made full provision for all those noble designs which, two years before, she and her husband had together devised. Immediately this was done she returned to the walks of active usefulness which had so long occupied her, and save that she carried a widow's heart as well as garb, she appeared like herself again. But even this last year of her life was by no means a year of rest from projects of Christian work, and when death so suddenly called her, the plans and funds for a new parsonage for the Centenary Church were engaging her most earnest attention.

The last few months of life were marked by a rich development of religious experience. She shared largely in the refreshing influences which accompanied the labours of Messrs. Inskip and McDonald, in Hamilton, and the sojourn of Mr. and Mrs. Inskip in her house was, doubtless, a special pleasure and profit. So greatly was she strengthened that she, who for forty years never ventured beyond a few words in class in relating her Christian experience, was now seen rising in the public fellowship meeting and love-feast, to declare fully the saving grace of God. She had always been noted for her sympathy with the bereaved and afflicted. Wherever there was sickness or death she was a quiet, useful visitor and friend. One who had long been associated with Mr. Jackson in business had been called away. Early in the morning she started for the house of mourning, saying, as she went, " We know not how soon we may need some one to do this for us." Immediately she joined in making the needful preparations for the funeral ; and while engaged in this mournful work of love, her spirit heard the Master's call, and instantly dropping its clay tenement, passed from labour to reward. She entered into rest May 5th, 1875, aged 71 years 1 month and 18 days.

The character of this noble woman was, in many respects, the complement of that of her husband. While so much alike as to be perfectly congenial and harmonious, they seemed necessary to each other to fill out to the full the grand life which they lived. The very last moments of life were a striking illustration of this : the one was praying, the other working, when summoned so quickly to the better life.

She was a woman of great energy and tireless industry. Excellent taste, a keen sense of propriety, and a knowledge of human nature which almost infallibly discerned the motives of those with whom she had to deal, combined to guide her own works to almost invariable success, and to make her the most valuable friend in counsel we have ever known. Her great administrative ability, whether in the ordering of her domestic affairs or in the management of the various Christian enterprises in which she was engaged, gave her the most perfect command of every part of the work in hand.

She was a woman of the deepest domestic affections, and of the most kindly social disposition. In the exhibition of these she was never demonstrative. With her there was no latent insincerity, no ostentatious show of kindness, no fair speeches which could be suspected of even unconscious hypocrisy, of fine sentiment. From her lips the vulgar incense of flattery was never offered, and few would even dare to have offered it to her. But notwithstanding all this, those who knew her best understood well the deep earnest nature which lay beneath that quiet exterior.

Her treatment of her household servants was one of the finest examples of Christian conduct we have known. A parental solicitude for their temporal and spiritual welfare marked all her dealings with them. Perhaps no one ever ruled a household more diligently than she, but the very exercise of her authority taught her servants to respect themselves as they respected her. There were no menials in her employ, and we believe the characters of many young persons have been permanently formed for good while in her service.

There was something truly grand in the unwavering strength of her conscientious convictions. When you heard her say, " I don't care what they say, it is not right," you felt at once, that in the light of that clear moral intuition, the sophisms of all worldly wisdom and plausible policy lay exposed. She had inherited all the stern morality of her Puritan ancestors, and to her, duty was inviolable law. Such a nature, so strong, earnest, active, and yet womanly, we seldom find.

To us, the study of the lives and character of these servants of God has been a profit and pleasure. We have ventured to make this brief record, believing it to be a sacred duty to transmit the influence of their example to the coming generation. Theirs was no life severed from the ordinary providential ways of men. It was purely human in all its work and sympathies, human and yet Christian, and for its broad humanity all the more useful as an example to mankind.

A Sermon

PREACHED BY

THE REV. W. J. HUNTER.

A SERMON

PREACHED BY THE

REV. W. J. HUNTER,

In the Centenary Church, Hamilton,

On the occasion of the death of Edward Jackson, Esq.[*]

" Therefore let no man glory in men. For all things are yours ; Whether
Paul, or Apollos, or Cephas, or the world, or life, or death, or things
present, or things to come ; all are yours ; And ye are Christ's ; and
Christ is God's."— 1 CORINTHIANS iii. 21, 22, 23.

ST. PAUL'S resolution touching the life-work
given him by the Master is set forth in
the second verse of the previous chapter. " I determined not to know any thing among you, save
Jesus Christ and Him crucified." How firmly
he adhered to that resolution is strikingly instanced
in the case before us. Certain foolish rivalries had
sprung up in the Corinthian Church, occasioned by
the diversified talents of those who preached the

---

[*] On this occasion the audience assembled was perhaps the largest ever
gathered in this church. The other appointments of the Circuit were
withdrawn. Representatives of all denominations were present, and
friends from the surrounding country came, some of them fifteen miles.
It was a time long to be remembered.

3

Gospel amongst them. The partisans, first divided in judgment, were soon divided in spirit, and then became intemperate in language. " Every one saith, I am of Paul ; and I of Apollos ; and I of Cephas." Now certainly in this race for popularity Paul stood a fair chance to win ; but had he encouraged their party spirit he would have drawn off their affections from Christ instead of uniting them to Him in whom all hearts should centre. Therefore he comes promptly to the rescue, and unsparingly denounces the mischievous and unscriptural partialities of the Corinthians, laying down that eternal axiom of Gospel philosophy : " Neither is he that planteth anything, nor he that watereth ; but God that giveth the increase." And in my text he proclaims that, through Christ, all things are, by God's grant, made the property of true believers.

I shall endeavour, on this solemn occasion, to confirm your attachment to the Saviour of our departed father by a plain illustration of the several particulars of this charter of privilege. The Apostle presents his declaration first of all in the form of a comprehensive generality, " All things are yours," which has been appropriately paraphrased thus : " All things are subordinated to your use and benefit. It is a gracious promise vouchsafed to you that the whole assemblage of visible things, the entire succession of events in which you are interested and concerned, shall contribute to your benefit. The wisdom and goodness of God so orders everything, leads you through such a succession of beneficent intricacies, so fits the events of this year into the events of that, the chastisements of yesterday into the mercies of to-day, that in the end you shall not wish to have had anything altered. You will feel that you have had a property in creation, a property in providence, a property in the issues of all being—' All things are yours." '

But St. Paul will leave no ground for doubt or unbelief, and therefore rests not his declaration on this comprehensive generality, but proceeds to specify the items included in it. "Paul, Apollos, Cephas, the world, life, death, things present, things to come."

These items will find a place under the following general heads :—

I. Man.

II. Creation.

III. Providence.

I. Man is ours. Next to God himself, the highest of man's possessions is man. An eminent writer has said, " In every star that looks down from heaven, in every flower that opens its calix to the sun, in every tree laden with summer fruits, in every rill that falls down the mountain side, we see the wisdom and goodness and glory of God ; but what would this whole

creation be, with the fulness and variety of its phe-
nomena, but for man—the image of God, called of
God to leave on this created world the stamp of his
spirit, and the impression of his nature?" Yes, man
is ours. Paul, Apollos, Cephas—Punshon, Spurgeon,
Talmage—Newton, Locke, Bacon—all are ours. The
wisdom and learning of the past have come down to
us, so that to-day the mind of every scholar is rich
with the spoils of time. Its divines have preached
for *us*. Its poets have sung for *us*. Its men of
science have studied for *us*. And so also of the present. Ministers in the pulpit, laymen in the pew, the
professor in his chair, and the merchant prince in his
counting house—all are ours—with all their genius,
talent, wealth, and labour. The most eminent
amongst them is but a " steward of the mysteries and
manifold mercies of God," appointed by Him to dis-
pense them to His people : an earthen vessel in which
treasures are deposited by Him for our use. They
are Christ's servants, and our servants for Jesus' sake.

And yet, my brethren, this item of privilege and
possession, standing at the head of the list, seems to
be ours least of all. How feeble and uncertain is the
tenure by which we claim it. The " silver cord,"
brittle and unseen, is all that binds our friends to us
and the world. Accidents that no human forethought
can avert, diseases that no human skill can arrest,

surround our pathway and our resting-place by day and by night. And how often it happens that men of eminent usefulness are removed from the Church and the world just when, in human estimation, their presence and service are most required. Stricken down by disease, or caught up into heaven like Elijah, we cry after them in broken accents, " My father, my father, the chariot of Israel and the horsemen thereof."

At the family table is a vacant chair, in the pew is a vacant seat, in the prayer-meeting and the official meeting well-known words of counsel and encouragement are wanting. The bereavement of orphanage is ours, and we say of departed worth, " it is gone ; he is dead." But, friends, we are mistaken. The good never die. The body goes down like seed corn into the grave; the soul lives, and the influence and example remain to cheer and bless the world. Elijah was translated, but Elisha caught the falling mantle, and the sons of the prophets exclaimed, "The *spirit* of Elijah doth rest upon Elisha." St. Paul was put to death, but the doctrines he preached, the confession he witnessed, the example he left, and his victory over death, have come down through the long ages to us, and are felt in our hearts, and manifested in our lives, as vital, energetic, and controlling principles. "When the blood of Christian martyrs was poured out on the sands of Rome, their persecutors imagined that they had made an end of them and their doctrine. But that blood, washed into the Tiber, was carried by its waters into the sea, and by the sea into the ocean, and by its waves to every kingdom of the earth ; and thus became a type, not more of the spreading doctrines of Christianity than of the augmented and widely diffused influence of these holy men." So it is still. The family may lose a pious father, but they retain his influence and example. The Church may lose its best, most gifted, and most liberal supporters, but their influence and example remain as a priceless heritage. A double portion of their spirit descends upon some youthful and timid Elisha, and, snatching up the falling mantle, he smites the waters of Jordan, that he may pass over on dry land.

God's servants are ours. Edward Jackson is ours. Identified with the rise and progress of this city, known throughout our Israel, God spared him to a ripe old age. His intelligent, unaffected, and earnest piety ; his sterling integrity and Christian liberality, have stamped his memory with the seal of immortality. His example will go down on the page of history, and generations yet unborn will follow in the good man's footsteps.

II. Creation is ours. "The world." St. Paul seems impatient here. He searches after some term or expression to convey the fulness of his thought, and cries out abruptly, " the world is yours "—" the world and all its inhabitants, however excellent in gifts and graces, are your servants for Christ's sake." Human laws provide for the security of personal property, but God in His wisdom and goodness has so constituted society that no man can be independent of his fellows. Nor can any monopolize the creatures of God. The sun, moon, and stars ; the rain and the produce of universal nature, belong to rich and poor alike.

But it does seem to me that, in the distribution of wealth amongst His own people, God acts on certain fixed principles, chief amongst which is the one that our earthly possessions should never exceed our spiritual graces. No man is qualified to use wealth aright without a measure of piety commensurate with it. There can be no more beautiful sight on earth, and no more evident proof of the influence and power of religion than that which is presented in the prosperous career of a young man rising in the world, and at the same time retaining his integrity, his moral principle, his piety; "as humble and courteous and unassuming in his wealth as in his poverty." But one of the saddest sights on earth is to see a man as he rises in the scale of society forgetting the humble piety of his youth, ashamed of the Church of his fathers, and seeking for some genteel religion with no

blood-stained cross in it—some fashionable Church,
where sin, and the law, and hell, are seldom mentioned,
but where conscience is rocked into slumber by the lul-
laby of cold and lifeless formalism.   I speak to you to-
night, young men, from the grave of one who began at the
foot of the hill, and climbed inch by inch and foot by
foot till he reached the summit.   What was the secret
of his success?   " The fear of the Lord is the beginning of wisdom."   That was the starting point.
" Not slothful in business ; fervent in spirit ; serving
the Lord."   That was the life motto and regulating
principle.   To him was richly verified the promise,
" the world is yours," and *in* him was strikingly exem-
plified the injunction, " they that use this world, as
not abusing it."   Now I am not here to promise every
young man setting out in life a like success.   God
knows what measure of this world's goods is best for
each of us.   But I am here to promise that if you
" seek first the kingdom of God and His righteousness," if you are diligent and attentive to your calling,
if you live in obedience to all the laws by which you
are governed, if your Christian graces keep pace with
your temporal prosperity, and, if you possess talent
and capacity, wealth and honour and happiness are
yours as certainly as though you had them at your command this moment.   Let those of us from whom
wealth is withheld remember that " godliness with

contentment is great gain." Our "bread shall be given, and our water shall be sure." The world is ours, and it owes every honest Christian a living.

I now pass to touch on the main point.

III. Providence is ours. Dear friends, there *is* a superintending hand—a hand that not only controls the universe, but also directs the ways of private life and family circumstance—a Being without whose consent not even a sparrow falleth to the ground. All the dispensations of His providence are ours. These are grouped together in my text in the terms, "life, death, things present, things to come."

The term life, as used in this passage, means present existence. Life has furnished a theme for endless productions. The philosopher, the orator, the moralist, and the poet, have all attempted a solution of the question, "What is your life?" Ask the philosopher and he will tell you that it is one of the deepest mysteries of metaphysical science. Ask the orator, and in the loftiest flights of imagination he will picture life as a stage on which men are the actors and the hosts of heaven the spectators. Ask the moralist, and his sage reply is, "Life is that which we measure by our sorrows, and note by its loss." Ask the poet, and he will answer by breathing forth in solemn strains its rapid flight and deep uncertainty. Would you find a satisfactory answer to the question, you must

consult this Book of Books, this key of knowledge.
It teaches us that life is a portion of infinite duration
—the vestibule of eternity—the soul's discipline for
immortality. What is the value of life? Go, ask
yon spirit, hopeless, ruined, lost. O! ask him quickly,
while the roar of the eternal ocean falls upon his ear ;
and the answer will come back in the words of the
dying queen, "*Millions of money for a moment of
time.*" Life has been fitly likened to a book. It has
a page for every day we live. Our actions, words,
and thoughts are all written in this book. When
life on earth terminates, the book is closed. In the
eternal world it will be given us again, and forever
we shall turn over its leaves and read their contents.
My brother, hast thou written aught in the book of
life that would paint thy cheek with a crimson blush
when read aloud in the presence of an assembled universe? Then haste thee now to Calvary, and place
thy book beneath the purple flood which streams from
the wounds of the Crucified, for this alone can obli-
terate the characters made with the pen of life.

These thoughts suggest another question. What is
the work of life? What its great mission? Is it to
heap up gold and silver as the dust? to possess broad
acres and stately dwellings? Ah, no! this is not *the*
work of life. Is it to acquire fame and renown? to
secure a name whose heroic deeds shall be wafted from

sea to sea and from shore to shore? No, this is not *the* work of life. The great work of life is to so cultivate the faculties of intellect and soul that when our present existence terminates we may be prepared for the society and enjoyments of heaven. There is a blissful or an awful eternity before each one of us. Immortality is stamped upon every human soul. The sweet flowers that open at your feet must wither, fade, and die. The charming landscape that spreads out before you the beauties of nature, must mingle with the ashes of a burning world. The day is approaching when "the heavens shall pass away with a great noise, and the elements shall melt with fervent heat, the earth also, and the works that are therein, shall be burned up." But the soul will survive this universal ruin, and remain imperishable amidst the flames of the universe. And yet it must—Spirit of the living God fasten the truth upon every conscience—at last be shut in with God, or be banished from His presence, an exile from glory and a traitor to the cross.

The soul is fallen, deeply fallen. Sin runs through its every ramification, but, thank God, it has been redeemed; it may be regenerated, and, clothed with righteousness divine, it may scale the mount of God and bask undazzled in the refulgent splendours of Deity. Now put all these facts together and you have an answer to the question, What is life's mission? Take first the fact that man is a sinner and unfit for heaven. Secondly, the fact that through the mediation of Christ he may be pardoned and saved. Thirdly, the fact that only in this present life is salvation attainable; and lastly, the fact that if not saved in time he must be lost forever, and as a rational and intelligent being you are constrained to confess that—

> "Nothing is worth a thought beneath
> But how I may escape the death
>   That never, never dies;
> How make mine own election sure,
> And when I fail on earth, secure
> A mansion in the skies."

But this is not all. It is not enough that I save my own soul. I am placed in this world as a member of the wide-spread human family. The law of God requires of me that I shall "love my neighbour as myself." It is the duty of every man to employ time and talent and money in seeking to save the lost and rescue the perishing. O, men of the world, why build on a foundation of sand? Why embrace shadows so soon to be dissipated? Why, O why, with the grave open at your feet, rush on heedless and regardless of the undecaying glory, honour, and immortality set before you in the Gospel. Brethren in the Lord, our day of labour is short and rapidly receding. Every badge of mourning, every funeral we attend, all that we hear and all that we see, unite to give emphasis to the admonition of God's word. "Whatsoever thy hand findeth to do, do it with thy might; for there is no work, nor device, nor knowledge, nor wisdom, in the grave, whither thou goest."

"Death" is ours. Properly speaking there is no death. What we call death is simply a change in our mode of existence. Death has become the gloomy thing it is on account of its consequences and associations.

Take as the first and principal of these, *the dissolution of the body*. Examine the human body; the bones, the muscles, the nerves, the circulation of the blood, the organs of sight, speech, and hearing. Consider the adaptation of each member to the use intended, and you will feel the force of the Psalmist's exclamation, "I am fearfully and wonderfully made." And there is something sad in the dissolution of this beautiful piece of mechanism. And then again, death dissolves all earthly relationships. It separates husbands and wives, parents and children, friends and acquaintances. In short, death is an enemy. "The last enemy that shall be destroyed is death."

And yet, strange at first sight, death finds a place in this inventory of Christian possessions. The Apostle calls death a privilege. Do you wish that he had left this item out of the charter? Nay, my brethren, be not too hasty in arriving at such a conclusion.

Consider that death is to the Christian a conquered foe, a vanquished enemy. Consider that to him it is the end of trial and of conflict, and you will appreciate the gift, and realize the full meaning of the Apostle when he says, " death is yours." Yours to conduct to the gates of glory, yours to clothe in the garments of immortality, yours as the end of labour, the end of sorrow, the end of sin. Go weep at the grave of buried love, if you will, but weep as the Christian poet wept when he said :—

" But we have parted, sister, thou art dead,
   On its last resting-place I laid thy head ;
   Then by thy coffin-side knelt down and took
   A brother's farewell kiss and farewell look.
   Those marble lips no kindred kiss returned ;
   From those veiled orbs no glance responsive burned.
   Ah ! then I felt that thou hadst passed away,
   That the sweet face I gazed on was but clay ;
   And then came memory with her busy throng
   Of tender images forgotten long.
   Years hurried back, and as they swiftly rolled,
   I saw thee, heard thee as in days of old.
   Sad, and more sad, each sacred feeling grew,
   Manhood was moved and sorrow claimed her due ;
   Thick, thick and fast the burning tear-drops started,
   I turned away and felt that we had parted.
   But not forever ; in the silent tomb
   Where thou art laid, thy kindred shall find room ;
   A little while, a few short years of pain,
   And one by one we'll come to thee again.
   The kind old father shall seek out the place,
   And rest with thee, the youngest of his race ;
   The dear, dear mother, bent with age and grief,

Shall lay her head by thine in sweet relief,
Sister and brother, and that faithful friend,
True from the first and tender to the end,
All, all in His good time who placed us here
To live, to love, to die and disappear,
Shall come and make their quiet bed with thee
Beneath the shadow of that spreading tree ;
With thee to sleep through death's long dreamless night,
With thee rise up and bless the morning light."

" Things present " are ours. At first sight we are somewhat perplexed as to the true interpretation of this expression. The idea seems to be embodied in the terms life, and the world, but a little attention will clear away the difficulty. By the terms life and the world, we are to understand the period of our probation, and the supply of our daily wants. And as the phrase, " things present," is used in contrast with the phrase, " things to come," it evidently means all the vicissitudes connected with life and the world. All the particulars of life, all the changes it may experience, all its pleasures and pains, trials and comforts, are ours. They are all over-ruled for our benefit, and " *all* things work together for good to them that love God."

" Things to come " are ours. I frankly confess my inability to picture the world of meaning contained in these three short words, "things to come." Even Paul himself, with all his eloquence, and all his inspi-

ration, could not do it. Caught up into the third
heaven, looking at its matchless beauty, and hearing
its marvellous melody, he comes back to earth, not to
gratify our curiosity, but to say that he " heard un-
speakable words, which it is not lawful for a man to
utter." And yet, my friends, we are not left in utter
ignorance of the world beyond. Heaven is revealed
to us as a great reality. It is "a better country,"
"a city that hath foundations." Our "Father's house,"
" the throne of God and the Lamb." Its inhabitants
" can die no more." " They shall hunger no more,
neither thirst any more, neither shall the sun light on
them, nor any heat; for the Lamb who is in the
midst of the throne shall feed them, and shall lead
them to living fountains of water, and God shall wipe
away all tears from their eyes." Precious Bible.
Glorious, peerless Christianity, thou art the only lamp
lighting up the " valley of the shadow of death." We
shrink back from annihilation. We feel and know
that we must live forever, and we long for the certain
knowledge of a resting-place into which the soul may
be received after the shipwreck of the body is over.
Where can we find such a refuge? Who amongst all
the wise men of earth can impart this certain knowledge? I search the world's library and question the
learning of the ages. I address myself to Cyrus, edu-

cated in the schools of the most illustrious Persian sages. Tell me, Cyrus,—

> "Are there no bowers, no lov'd retreats,
> Remote from sin, from sorrow free?
> Eternal calm, eternal day,
> Tell me, O tell, if such there be?"

Mark his answer. "I cannot imagine that the soul lives only as long as it remains in this mortal body, and ceases to live when it is separated from it. I am rather inclined to think it will then have more intelligence and greater purity."

Rather inclined to think. That is all he knows about it. I address myself to Socrates. See! Socrates is dying. Come near and catch the last words of the great man. He is speaking to his friends : " I go to die, you to live; which of us goes the best way is known to God alone."

Enough of the schools. I question Paul. He approaches me with beaming eye and uplifted look, exclaiming, " O death, where is thy sting? O grave, where is thy victory?" " For we *know* that if our earthly house of this tabernacle were dissolved, we have a building of God, an house not made with hands eternal in the heavens." But, tell me, Paul, what is the ground of this boasted confidence? Is it thy logical acumen, thy speculative knowledge acquired in Tarsus and at the feet of Gamaliel? No, no; Paul

4

refers not to these, but rather to the word of One who cannot lie. One who, to evidence that death cannot retain his victim forever, approached the sepulchre of the dead and called him back to life. Yea, he grounds his assertion on the word of One who, by His own resurrection from the dead, destroyed death and him that had the power of death, and encouraged his followers with the words, "In my father's house are many mansions. If it were not so I would have told you." " My father's house." O, brethren, this is no shadow filling in the horizon. It is a place —a house—a home where friend meets friend—where there is love and joy and peace forevermore.

But we must not overlook the *doctrine* of the text. These rich possessions are the heritage of believers, by virtue of their union with Christ. Read the Apostle : " Christ is God's." This is the first link, and it takes hold of the throne. " Ye are Christ's." This is the second link. And because ye are Christ's, and Christ is God's, and God is infinite, " all things are yours."

In accordance with the life-long feelings and oft-expressed sentiments of our departed father, and out of deference to the expressed wishes of surviving relatives, I am debarred the privilege of recounting the many amiable and praiseworthy traits of character which marked his happy, prosperous, and useful life. To those who knew him such a task were needless.

His life is before you. Some of you have read it daily for many years. If you ask me again for the secret of its prosperity and sunshine, my answer is, " Trust in the Lord and do good ; so shalt thou dwell in the land, and verily thou shalt be fed." " Wait on the Lord and keep His way, and He shall exalt thee to inherit the land." " Mark the perfect man and behold the upright ; for the end of that man is peace." If you would have such a life and such a death, "trust in the Lord and do good." That is the whole secret. If I may not dwell upon his life, I am at liberty to speak of his death. What a beautiful death was Edward Jackson's ! It was more like a translation than like death. In his own parlour, surrounded by his wife and a few intimate friends—his favourite hymns had been sung by one of his favourite singers— the company had knelt in prayer, when, suddenly, " he was not, for God took him." I visited him on that beautiful Sabbath evening. The family had not yet returned from church, and he was alone, sitting in the library. The gas was not lighted, and as he rose to welcome me, he said, " I am musing in the twilight, thinking of Jesus and heaven." After stating, in answer to my inquiries, that he had passed a pleasant day, entirely free from pain, and from the spasms of the heart which recently had distressed him, he added, " But, Brother Hunter, I have an impression that the end is near; all the day I have seemed as though floating in the atmosphere." Just then the friends to whom I have alluded came in, and I left the house to visit another death chamber.

My colleague, the Rev. Mr. Benson, was one of the company, and Mr. Jackson said, " Light the gas in the parlour, and Bro. Benson will sing some of the songs of Zion; it will be beautiful thus to close up the day."

All sat down in the parlour, save Mr. Sanford, his son-in-law, who sat just outside the front door in the cool of the evening. When about to kneel, Mr. Jackson said to the latter, whom he regarded with all a father's affection and tenderness, always calling him by the familiar name Willie : " Now, Willie, come in to prayer." These were the last words addressed to earth. Mr. Benson had proceeded some way in his devotions, praying that if consistent with the Divine will this valuable life might be spared, when he added, " But whatever the result may be, suffer no cloud to come between Thee and Thy servant's soul." Mr. Jackson responded audibly, "Amen," and that moment fell from his knees and was supported in the arms of a friend. Medical aid was instantly summoned, but it was useless. The happy spirit had

> " Taken its last triumphant flight
> From Calvary's to Zion's height."

He did not see death—there was no conflict, no struggle, no bitter agony. He slept in Jesus, and his features wore the same sweet smile, which always made him a welcome guest in the social and religious circle. Who will take his place? Who will grasp the fallen banner, and bear it to such a death?

> " O may *I* triumph so
> When all my warfare's past,
> And dying find my latest foe
> Under my feet at last."

A SERMON

PREACHED BY

THE REV. JOHN POTTS.

A SERMON

REV. JOHN POTTS.

In the Centenary Church, Hamilton,

On the occasion of the death of Mrs. Edward Jackson.

"_____"

MAN, wherever found and however cultured
and circumstanced, is a being of desire. D
is _____ of ____, and the ____ ___ ___
are largely affected by his _____ and _____
As he rises in the scale of intellectual and moral
manhood, his desire rises and becomes more enlarged
and worthy of him. Desire, according to character,
may be animal, intellectual, and spiritual. Christianity has enlarged and exalted human desire—
has lifted it to a higher altitude, and greatly extended
its vision and objects. Christianity has done more
than beget and increase spiritual desire, for it has
furnished the wherewith to satisfy its largest and
increased longings. The revelations of the Christian

A SERMON

PREACHED BY THE

REV. JOHN POTTS,

In the Centenary Church, Hamilton,

On the occasion of the death of Mrs. Edward Jackson.

"But now they desire a better country, that is, a heavenly."—HEB. xi. 16.

MAN, wherever found and however cultured and circumstanced, is a being of desire. It is characteristic of him, and its nature and extent are largely affected by his character and condition. As he rises in the scale of intellectual and moral manhood, his desire rises and becomes more enlarged and worthy of him. Desire, according to character, may be animal, intellectual, and spiritual. Christianity has enlarged and ennobled human desire— has lifted it to a higher altitude, and greatly extended its vision and objects. Christianity has done more than beget and increase spiritual desire, for it has furnished the wherewith to satisfy its largest and intensest longings. The revelations of the Christian system are designed to accomplish this. Humanity is ignorant and desires instruction; and Christianity furnishes light and knowledge on these great problems which pertain to sin and salvation—to probation and immortality. Humanity is guilty, depraved, and comfortless, and desires a God to meet such necessities. Christianity reveals a God just adapted—a personal God—a forgiving God—an indwelling God —a God of all consolation. Humanity is immortal, and, therefore, has desires that overleap the confines of probation and penetrate the future; and Christianity meets these God-implanted desires with revelations of the rest that remains for the people of God, and of the inheritance that is incorruptible and undefiled, and that fadeth not away. Place man where you may, furnish all that earth can afford and all of earth that he can enjoy, he must go out after something better and higher—something in harmony with his redeemed and immortal instincts. Like those spoken of in the text, he will desire a better country.

Our theme to-night is Heaven.—A more glorious subject cannot occupy human thought. The heaven of the Bible has many attractions for all those that confess themselves strangers and pilgrims, and that can testify, " We are journeying unto the place of which the Lord has said, ' I will give it you.' "

Concerning the house of many mansions, the prepared place and the glorious city, this Book reveals much that is encouraging to faith and hope. Yet there is a certain reticence relative to the future maintained from the Genesis to the Revelations of this sacred volume. Many questions come to us and are propounded by us to which there is no authoritative response. Where is heaven? I cannot define its locality in the universe; I cannot describe the geography of that better country. How do the disembodied exist and recognize each other? It is hard for us whose ideas of existence and recognition are all identified with the terrestrial and the material, to know how they live and hold fellowship with each other. Are they familiar with what occurred on earth? Do those who go carry tidings of those left behind? Do they speak of us, who so often think and speak of them? You are all interested in the theme of our text, because there is not one here who has not relations and friends in the land of pure delight. We are all interested, because of our personal relations to a future state. I need hardly state the reason for selecting these passages. You are all familiar with the mysterious Providential dispensation that bows you to-night with no common grief, and yet somehow makes you feel that heaven is not far away. That visitation causes you to think of heaven, and causes me to preach upon the subject on this memorial occasion. From the scene and surroundings of death "the elect lady" was translated to the scenes and surroundings of immortal life and glory. From the sympathizing and ungrudging services of pure Christian benevolence, the handmaid of the Lord was summoned to the higher service and reward of the heavenly state. It is difficult for some of us to realize that we shall never look upon that familiar face again; that we shall never hold converse with that truest of friends; that we shall never hear her speak, as was her wont, of the Centenary Church, of the Orphan Asylum, and of the sick and sorrowing. Who can think of this sanctuary without being reminded of the name of JACKSON? For it she worked, as many here know right well; in it she worshipped, in the beauty of holiness; in its impressive services she was made heavenly-minded; and from yonder pew she looked up and desired, with intensity of desire, the better country, that is, the heavenly. With her and many others that I could mention, whose cherished names now pass before my mind, heaven is not an object of desire. The life-long desire of Christian character on earth is now realized, and they are present with the Lord. It is to us that the beautiful words of the text are applicable. May they be the sentiment

of every heart in this vast assembly: "But now
they desire a better country, that is, a heavenly."
Noble desire, worthy of man! A better country
than the land of promise—than the land flowing
with milk and honey? Where is it? Not on earth
—only in heaven. Of heaven as a country we are
to speak; and as the text involves the idea of com-
parison, we must treat it accordingly. May meditation of heaven make us heavenly, so that it can be
said of us—"But now they desire a better country,
that is, a heavenly." I will first present a few
considerations to justify the description of heaven as
a better country; and will then show that to reach
that heavenly country is the desire of every Christian.

I. LET ME JUSTIFY THE DESCRIPTION HERE GIVEN
OF HEAVEN. Illustration rather than argument is
what will best elucidate the meaning of the text.
(1) *Heaven is better because it is the antetype.*
Canaan was a defective type of heaven. It failed,
in many essential particulars, to typify the heavenly
land of promise. But for ages, in the grand and
poetical teaching of the Church, it has been regarded
as a type of the better country, and as such we must
review it. All types are of less importance and
value than their antetype. This is clearly taught
in the relation of Judaism to Christianity. The
sacrifices of the law, the high priest of the law,

the services of the law were all inferior to the One
glorious sacrifice, which is perpetually efficacious, to
the High Priest of our profession, and to the more
simple and spiritual service of the Christian dispensation. This principle of interpretation may be
applied to the earthly and heavenly Canaan. The
heavenly Canaan is as much better as the spiritual
is better than the temporal. It is as much better
as the heavenly is better than the earthly—the immortal better than the transitory. (2) *Heaven is
a better country because of its safety from foes.*
When the Israelites, under the leadership of Joshua,
entered the promised land, they found it inhabited
by tribes and nations hostile on national and religious
grounds. They were opposed at every point, and
had to fight and conquer to have the undisturbed
possession of the land. Like the earthly Canaan,
this world is not free from foes to goodness and to
grace. The believer is taught most clearly that
there are foes visible and invisible. These enemies
war against the soul—against the soul's safety, holiness, and happiness. If there be no antagonists,
where is the need for such counsel as that urged
by the Apostle: " Put on the whole armour of God,
fight the good fight of faith, endure hardness as good
soldiers of Jesus Christ?" It is never safe in this
territory to be found without the armour. There is

no security while here against attacks, and there
is no certainty as to the time, the place, or the mode
of attack. All spiritual foes are subserviently leagued
with the chief enemy, "who goeth about like a
roaring lion, seeking whom he may devour." Martial
glory and the prospect of the laurels of victory may
cause men to pant for the sight of the foe and for
the excitement of the contest. So it has been, as
history attests. But the bravest veteran of the field
rejoices when the conflict is over and peace reigns
on all the borders. And so it is with the spiritual
army of Jesus, the Captain of our salvation. The
soldiers that compose it do not dread the field of
battle. They are often eager for the fight, because
the result is the extension of the Redeemer's kingdom among men; yet they exult in the sublime
prospect of a universal victory and a perpetual peace.
In this respect is not heaven a better country in
its absolute and eternal safety from foes? When
the spiritual pilgrims of the desert would pass over
the Jordan of death, it is not to enter a land inhabited by enemies; it is not to meet in conflict the
embattled hosts that must be conquered for the
possession of the heavenly inheritance. That better
country is indeed populated, but it is with friends
and kindred of the same family. There reside in
it the friend that sticketh closer than a brother—

the angelic friends innumerable who have manifested such sympathy in relation to the redemption and salvation of man—and then there are the redeemed from the earth, who are sharers with us of the favours and the grace of God. Surely, then, the description is justified—a better country. (3) *Heaven is a better country because of its freedom from sin and sorrow.* Delightsome as was that goodly land, fruitful as were its vine-clad hills, and refreshing as were its living streams, it was not free from sin, and could not exempt its inhabitants from sorrow. There, in the midst of covenant blessings, and in the presence of remarkable evidences of special divine regard, the people sinned against God—against the God who had delivered them from Egypt, guided them through the desert, and sustained them miraculously. They departed from God in cultivating an evil heart of unbelief, and in turning from the heaven-appointed worship to idolatry. Nor was that land free from sorrow. Wherever there is sin there must be sorrow and grief and suffering. The sorrow of affliction and of death darkened the Israelitish dwellings in the land flowing with milk and honey. If our thoughts be transferred from the Israelites in Canaan to the militant Church generally, in it we find both sin and sorrow. Sin is widespread, and of multiform manifestation. It disturbs, and often destroys, our harmony and peace; it touches life's holiest actions, and pollutes our best offerings. A poisonous malaria rises from every part of this sin-cursed world. If it be not the flagrant sin of commission, it is the God-dishonouring sin of omission. And there is also sorrow. It darkens all the land. At one time or other its shadows rest on every heart and on every home. This is a rule without an exception. " Man is born to trouble, as the sparks fly upward." It comes in all days, at all hours, and in all forms. Now it may be the sorrow of disappointment, when prospects are blighted and hopes lie crushed and bleeding. It may be the sorrow of separation :—

> " Friend after friend departs,
> Who has not lost a friend?
> There is no union here of hearts,
> That has not here an end."

It may be the sorrow of affliction which presses down the soul; or it may be that of bereavement. Whatever other sorrow we escape, none of us has been exempt from the sorrow that wrings the soul, when kindred—and friends as loved as kindred—are taken from us by the ruthless hand of death. In view of all these things, is not heaven a better country? There, there is freedom, absolute and eternal freedom from sin and sorrow. Nothing that defileth can

5

enter that perfect and holy place. The breath of sin never taints the celestial atmosphere. The voice of sin is never heard amid the pure harmonies of the skies. The loathsome and deformed wretch never walks the streets or enters the homes of the heavenly city. A region without a sinful thought, purpose, word, look, or act. All the inhabitants holy. There is no sorrow there. Every tear is wiped away. Every sigh of earth has been converted into a hallelujah of the skies. The emblems of sorrow are never seen in the wide range of that better country. The white-robed multitude are never attired in the weeds of mourning. Whiter than snow are their robes of blissful purity. The inhabitants never say that they are sick ; and death is unknown in that fadeless and graveless land. Heaven is surely better, since it is a sinless and sorrowless state. (4) *The description is justified in its more complete and unceasing enjoyments.* The blessedness of heaven is not all negation. That there were enjoyments in Canaan none can deny. Compared with Egypt and its bondage and drudgery, and the wilderness with its weary and desolate wanderings, the Land of Promise was indeed a joyous country. That the people of God now on earth have enjoyment, all must admit. There are earthly enjoyments, which belong to the natural : the joy of home and family

and friends—the joy of reception and communication. There are spiritual enjoyments, too: the joy
of relationship to God, of communion with God
and of fellowship with the people of God. While
all this is cheerfully acceded, it must be confessed
that the enjoyments of earth are liable to change
and to sad interruption. The cup of happiness may
be dashed to pieces from our very lips. To-day we
may be jubilant and satisfied, and to-morrow we may
be hushed and crushed with trouble and grief. The
joys of earth are mostly unsatisfying. They are
certainly short-lived; they flourish in the morning
and, not seldom, are withered in the evening.
Heaven is a better country, for its enjoyments are
both complete and increasing. There is no admix-
ture of the bitter with their sweetness. There is
no unhappy reflection following their most prolonged
participation. There is no interruption to their con-
stancy by the dark shadows of fear that trouble
is right at hand. Amid the spiritual festivity of
heaven's glorious banquet, no hand is seen upon
the wall, pencilling—" *Mene, mene, Tekel* "—God
hath numbered thy kingdom and finished it; thou
art weighed in the balances and found wanting.
The enjoyments of heaven are complete and perpetual. "In thy presence, there is fulness of joy;
and at thy right hand there are pleasures for ever-

more." The joy of eternal security is complete. The joy of perfect holiness and happiness is complete. The joy of a restful yet ceaseless and progressive activity is complete. The joy of recognition and companionship is complete. The sundered friends of other years have met in the unending re-union of heaven's bright and glorious home. The joy of being near and like Christ is complete. Christ is the full-orbed glory of the heavenly metropolis. In the renewed lustre of His light they shine. In His love they live and rejoice. On His glorified person they gaze with unutterable rapture until each of the innumerable multitude feels the same glorious sentiment—"Whom have I in heaven but thee." And the immortality of the whole renders this joy unceasing as well as satisfying. Nothing could compensate for the want of the certainty of immortality. Such want would darken heaven's light and hush the music and the song into the silence of an irrecoverable despair.

> " Oh ye blest scenes of permanent delight,
> Full above measure ! lasting beyond bound !
> A perpetuity of bliss is bliss.
> Could you so rich and raptured fear an end,
> That ghastly thought would drink up all your joy
> And quite unparadise the realms of light.
> O blessed Heaven ! Thou rest of the weary ! Thou
> Home of the pilgrim ! Thou inheritance of the saints !
> Thou sinless, painless, sorrowless, deathless
> Graveless land ; thou art indeed the better country."

II. WE PASS TO NOTICE BRIEFLY THAT TO REACH
THIS BETTER COUNTRY IS THE DESIRE OF ALL TRUE
CHRISTIANS. "But now they desire a better country."
(1) *It is a universal Christian desire.* However
Christians may differ on other matters—upon Church
government—upon docrines of theology—upon in-
strumental music in the service of the sanctuary—
they all agree in desire for the heavenly country.
It would be impossible to find a Christian pilgrim,
in any part of the world, not desiring the family
home of God's household. Go where you may,
wherever Christ is loved and trusted, heaven is desired. Whatever else is partial or peculiar among
Christian persons, and in various times and places,
the love and desire of the better country are universal
and constant in the household of faith. (2) *It is an
influential desire.* The desire of knowledge, of
position, of wealth, is influential. The desire of
heaven is influential also. It influences thought,
motive, conversation, and conduct. It is the desire
of heaven that leads men to pray, to believe, to
engage in those acts of mind and heart which tend
to prepare for heaven. Take away the desire of
heaven, and the energies of the Christian are at
once paralysed. He that has no desire of heaven for
himself has surely no desire that others may obtain
it. (3) *It is an evinced desire.* The desire of heaven

may be evinced by reading and speaking of it. Those that intend to visit a distant country gather information concerning it by reading and conversation. They will speak of its climate and government, of its inhabitants and scenery. They will read what has been written about it, to correct their errors and to enlarge their appreciation. Christians speak to each other about the heavenly country. They read with peculiar interest all that is written about its Government and King; about its population, angelic and redeemed, and about its associations and privileges. *This desire is evinced by going to it as a permanent home.* The desire is not all that it ought to be if it be evinced only in reading and speaking of heaven. Heavenly desire evinces itself by the actual journey of the pilgrim of Zion. It is as they go that they read and talk of it, and invite others to join them: " Come, then, with us, and we will do thee good, for the Lord hath spoken good concerning Israel."

Heaven is not far off—not far to the eye of faith. You are nearing it; you shall enter it. What a change from earth to heaven! from probation to immortality! When shall it come? Who can tell? Our departed friend had no intimation of the change that was to be her experience in the twinkling of an eye. I cannot tell you of her dying testimonies

to the presence, power, and preciousness of Christ
to sustain and make triumphant. Had weeks of
suffering been appointed her, we might have golden
sentences of peaceful and victorious testimony to
present, but not a word was spoken. What then?
I point you to her life as an illuminated record of
Christian and benevolent service—a record of three
and forty years. Her end was eminently characteristic. The sudden call found her engaged in her
Master's business. Edward Jackson died praying,
and his devoted widow died, or rather was translated
from the exercises of Christian sympathy and work
to enter the rest and reward of heaven. On the
morning of the last day of Mrs. Jackson's life she
conducted family worship, as had been her custom
since the removal of Mr. Jackson to the skies. Her
prayer on that occasion was wonderful in its fer-
vency of spirit, and in its comprehensiveness. The
members of the household were deeply impressed and
awed by a sacred sense of God's presence. It would
seem as though she was admitted to a special near-
ness of access at that her last season of domestic
worship. I feel to-night as a mourning son, having
lost in Mrs. Jackson one of my best and dearest
friends. While a seat among yonder mourners would
most accord with my feelings, I confess that it is
a comfort to me to be here, and to have taken part

in the funeral of our dear departed mother in Israel. I was not so favoured when God was pleased to call Mr. Jackson. Just before leaving home for a voyage over the Atlantic, I received a letter, I think about the last he ever wrote, in which he expressed the hope of recovery, but if not, the hope that I would follow on and overtake him in the heavenly home. When tidings of his death reached me, I was standing in front of City Road Chapel, in London, only a few yards from the grave of Wesley. I felt then a deep regret that I had left this country, and was thus hindered from paying my respects to one of the best men I ever knew. As I stood there, three thousand miles from home, I remembered how he told me, while I was pastor of this Church, that he regarded it a special favour from the Lord to be called home suddenly. It seemed to me that God gratified the desire of his faithful servant. Our dear and glorified friend, Mrs. Jackson, did not express a wish for death, but had a great dread of living to be a burden to any one. She felt not suffering; she saw not death; but ceased at once to work and live. I address not only mourning kinsfolk, but a mourning Church to-night. What shall I say *to you?* To the relatives I say, see that her interest in God's cause—whether of his Church or his poor—be reproduced in your character and lives. To the sisterhood of this Church, who feel to-night without a leader, I would say, "That ye be not slothful, but followers of her who, through faith and patience, inherits the promises." Take up the work where she left it; and, like your long-acknowledged leader, when you die, die at your post. What shall I say to the unconverted, and, therefore, the unprepared for death? This is the source of the dispensation to you, "Thus saith the Lord—set thy house in order, for thou shalt die and not live."

Lines in Memory

OF

MRS. LYDIA ANN JACKSON.

Lines in Memory of

MRS. LYDIA ANN JACKSON.

BY MISS S. J. WHITE.

IS she dead? Is the wheat-ear dead,
   Laid low by the reaper's blade?
Is it dead, though the leaves were doomed so soon
   To fall and fade?

Is it dead? Thrown into the ground
   In silence to decay?
Is it dead, though it lie there buried deep
   For many a day?

Is it dead? When the whole earth rings
   With the greeting of the spring,
It will rise with joy to obey the call—
   A beauteous thing.

When its lovely petals fade,
   That the fruit may swell and grow,
Is the flower dead, though its transient bloom
   Wither below?

Is this death? and is *she* dead
　Whom we lately missed from earth?
Is this the end of a noble life
　Of matchless worth?

Ah no! let the wheat decay;
　For we see in the future years
Great harvest fields all covered o'er
　With golden ears.

And let the sweet flowers fall
　Like flakes of summer snow;
The fruit will be sweeter, richer far
　Than we can know.

The Christian knows no death,
　Though the earthly life decay.
Death! 'Tis the breaking of a bright
　And glorious day.

A holy woman's name
　Lives on, and can never die
Wherever her sympathy has dried
　A mourner's eye.

She lives where her prayers have raised
　A soul to a higher life;
Wherever her gentle, loving words
　Have banished strife.

She lives in the many souls
　By her bright example led,
Who are following close her footsteps now.
　She is not dead!

She lives ! ah, best of all !
　She lives with Christ above ;
Where naught can ever mar her peace
　Or quench her love.

She lives far, far beyond
　The reach of mortal eye.
" Death, where's thy sting ? "　The saved of God
　Can *never* die.

HAMILTON, *Ont.*

The following fine hymn is that referred to in the memoir, as the last one which Mr. Jackson joined in singing ere his spirit took its flight to join in the songs of the sanctuary on high.

THE POWER OF PRAYER.

Moderato.

G. F. ROOT.

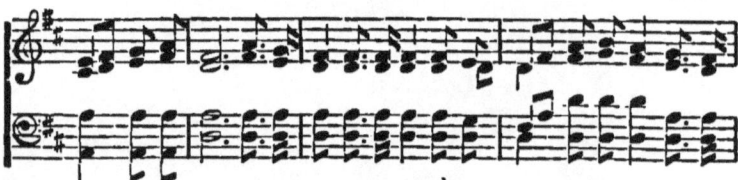

Chorus.

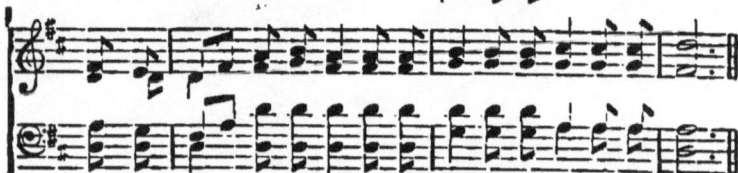

1 When my soul was distress'd, and my spirit was bow'd,
   And the dark waves of trouble ran wild;
   Then I pray'd to the Lord and He parted the cloud,
   And He look'd down upon me and smil'd.

Chorus.—Oh the sunshine drove darkness away,
   And freed my glad heart from its pall;
   And I wish'd, oh I wish'd that the whole world would pray
   For the smile of the Lord on us all.

2 When my friends had all left me alone to my lot,
   Then I went to my Saviour and Friend;
   And He soothingly spake to my spirit, "Fear not;
   I am with thee e'en unto the end."

3 When billows of sorrow did over me roll,
   Then I pray'd for His help from above;
   And He looked down upon me and filled up my sonl
   With emotions of rapturous love.

The following letter was kindly handed to me by the Rev. Mr. Potts, after these "MEMORIALS" had gone through the press. So far as I know, it was the last letter Bro. Jackson ever wrote. It speaks for itself. It will no doubt be read with profit by the numerous friends of the deceased, as it has been by

THE PUBLISHER.

HAMILTON, June 28th, 1872.

MY DEAR BRO. POTTS—

Your kind and sympathising letter of the 26th is received, and is refreshing to my thirsty soul. I am truly under the chastising hand of my Heavenly Father. It is in great pain and with much difficulty that I write these few lines. I will tell you briefly the nature of my affliction. I was at St. Paul, with Mrs. J. and Emma Spencer, partly on a visit and partly on business, when I was taken with a chill ; and in taking a sweat, I got slightly burnt on the left limb, a little below the hip-joint. I travelled home with it in that condition, and it got irritated ; and when I commenced to poultice, it developed into a frightful ulcer, of great virulence, giving me much pain, so as to deprive me of sleep and appetite, and in the end it may have a fatal issue. But I am thankful to say, my dear Brother, that I feel myself to be in the hands of a merciful and kind Father, who sustains me in my severe trial, and who, I doubt not, will bring me through, whether by life or death, all the better for having passed through the furnace. This is my desire, and for this I pray. My dear wife has a heavy trial in nursing me, but she seems endued with strength for the occasion. She is in good health, and wishes to be kindly remembered to you, Mrs. Potts, and the dear children ; likewise to Dr. Douglas and family.

I am glad to hear that you are going, for the recuperation of your worn-out powers, over the old Atlantic, and that you and your friend, Dr. Douglas, will be companions on the voyage. May you have a prosperous voyage and a safe return. If it is the will of my Father, I hope I may be here to hail your return ; if otherwise, overtake me in that

" Land of pure delight,
Where saints immortal reign."

Again, with kindest love to Maggie and the children, and with reiterated wishes for your continued prosperity in things temporal and things eternal, I bid you adieu.

Your affectionate Brother,

EDWARD JACKSON.